Questions are the Answers

*To Barbara Pease
who can turn coal
into diamonds*

Questions are the Answers

HOW TO GET TO 'YES' IN NETWORK MARKETING

ALLAN PEASE

Manjul Publishing House

First published in India by

MANJUL

Manjul Publishing House

- 7/32, Ansari Road, Daryaganj, New Delhi 110 002
Website: www.manjulindia.com

Registered Office:
10, Nishat Colony, Bhopal 462 003 - India

Distribution Centres
Ahmedabad, Bengaluru, Bhopal, Kolkata, Chennai,
Hyderabad, Mumbai, New Delhi, Pune

Questions are the Answers - How to get to Yes in Network Marketing
by *Allan Pease*

Published by agreement with
PEASE INTERNATIONAL PTY. LTD. AUSTRALIA,

Edited by Lisa Tierney, Ray & Ruth Pease, Daniel Le Roux

Layout by Karen Stirling

© 2000 by Allan Pease
All rights reserved.

This edition first published in 2001
Twenty-sixth impression 2017

**This edition is authorized for sale in the Indian Subcontinent
(India, Pakistan, Sri Lanka, Bangladesh, Nepal, Bhutan & Myanmar)**

ISBN   978-81-86775-05-9

Printed and bound in India by Replika Press Private Limited

Contents

Introduction

LUKE AND MIA

Luke was a builder who was determined to make his business a financial success. His wife Mia was an accountant who was loved by her clientèle. One day their neighbour Martin invited them to attend a meeting and hear about a business opportunity. Martin didn't give much detail about it but the meeting was just a few doors away and they liked him, so they decided to go. Besides, they'd probably meet some new neighbours.

As the meeting progressed, Luke and Mia couldn't believe what they were seeing and hearing. They saw a Network Marketing plan that gave them the opportunity to achieve financial freedom and a level of success beyond their imagination. They couldn't stop talking about it for several days. They decided to get started because, they thought, "surely **everyone** who saw the plan will want to join!"

But it wasn't as simple as they thought. Not everyone seemed to have the same enthusiasm for it as they did, some people didn't even turn up to their meetings to hear about it and some of their closest friends wouldn't even give them an appointment. Despite this, they gradually built a solid business. But it wasn't going as fast as they would have liked.

"Just imagine," Luke said to Mia, "if people could tell us why they **should** join Network Marketing instead of us trying to convince them. If only there was such a way..."

There is a way - and this book will show you that way.

The biggest fear that most people have about entering Network Marketing is that they will need to be high-powered sales people to reach the top levels. This book contains a simple system that will allow you to recruit new people with relative ease. There are no tricks, just techniques and principles that will work - provided you do.

Why I Wrote this Book

When I was first introduced to Network Marketing in 1980, I was amazed that such a tremendous opportunity could exist that was simple, legal, ethical, fun and lucrative. And it wasn't just another 'get-rich-quick-scheme'- it was a 'get rich' **system.**

For 10 years prior, I had been researching and developing communication and sales techniques that had added zeros to corporate bottom lines and turned people into millionaires. I thought, "Wow! If I could introduce these highly success-ful techniques into Network Marketing, the results could be mind-boggling!"

This book is the result of years of adapting, modifying, test-ing and applying the techniques to Network Marketing. You will discover simple, easy to learn skills that will propel you along the path to great success as thousands of others, just like you, are discovering right now.

And the great thing about it is that you don't have to change what you have already learned from your upline. With around 2 hours of study and some dedicated practice you can start growing your business to a level that will astound you.

The Promise

There's a promise that goes with the system you will learn in this book.

> *If you promise to learn the*
> *technique by heart and not*
> *to change a word for the first 14 days,*
> *I promise that the results will be*
> *beyond your wildest dreams.*

Now that's a pretty big promise, isn't it? But it's also a two-way deal – I want you to promise to practice, practice and practice until you can repeat the words in your sleep. No ifs, buts or maybes – just an unwavering dedication to learning the technique. This way it will become permanently yours. A wide range of other business ventures to which I have been an adviser, consultant or partner, have made **hundreds of millions** of dollars, recruited **thousands** of new members to their causes and increased their bottom line by **20%, 50%, 100%, 500%** and **1,000%** using this system. These are not exaggerated claims. What you will learn here can dramatically change your life but you must agree to stick to the system. If you agree, say **YES**, aloud, right now.

If you didn't say **YES** aloud, go back to the beginning of this page and read it again.

Note: where the word 'he' is used it applies equally to men and women. If there are gender differences in behaviour, this will be specified.

YOUR PERSONAL TURBO-CHARGER

There are so many excellent books and tapes available on

how to make appointments and how to present the business plan that these subjects will not be covered here in any depth. This book shows you exactly what to do, what to say and how to say it to get good prospects to say 'yes' in face to face meetings.

The information here is intended to turbo-charge your presentations **without** alteration to what you already know. For this reason most of the emphasis in the book will be on the second key, **'Find the Hot Button'.**

Never change what works – turbo-charge it!

Allan Pease

Section 1

The First Step

Like most things in life, few people can look at the drawing at the start of this section and see its obvious message. To the untrained eye, it's just a series of unrelated lines that make little sense. But when you learn how to read between the lines, you'll realise that you just needed to adjust your perspective a little to discover the answer. And that's exactly what we'll teach you to do in this book. (Angle this page down and away from you and close one eye.)

THE FIVE GOLDEN RULES FOR SUCCESS

At the tender age of eleven, I was asked to sell household sponges to help raise money to build a hall for my scout troop. The scoutmaster, a wise old man, divulged a secret to me; I call it **the law of consequence.** I have lived by this law and I guarantee that anyone who practices it must eventually succeed. I'll give you this law exactly as I received it – 'Success is a game – the more times you play the more times you win. And the more times you win the more successfully you'll play.'

Let's Apply This Rule to Networking-

'The consequence of asking more people to join you is that more people will join you – the more times you ask them to join you, the better you become at asking.' In other words, you need to ask lots of people to join you.

RULE # 1 SEE MORE PEOPLE

This is the most important rule. Talk to anyone who will stand still long enough to listen to you. Don't become a prospecting snob or a card shuffler who tries to psych good prospects out of the deck. If you find yourself looking through your prospect list and saying, "... they're too old ... too young ... too rich ... too poor ... too remote ... too smart..." etc, etc, then you're heading down a track that leads to failure. In the early stages of building your business you need to talk to everyone because you need the practice. When you talk to everyone about your business, the law of averages proves that you will be successful, it's just a matter of **how** successful. There is no problem that you'll ever have in your business that can't be solved by increased activity. If you feel depressed about where your life is going, simply double your number of presentations. If your business isn't building as quickly as you want, increase your output. Increased activity is a cure-all for most of the worries you'll ever have. **Talk to everyone**. That's the First Rule.

RULE # 2 SEE MORE PEOPLE

Keep calling people. You can be the best presenter in town but if you don't see enough prospects, you're out of business. You can be an excellent dresser and have a great personality, but without a significant volume of presentations, you'll only ever be average. Talk to everyone.

RULE # 3 SEE MORE PEOPLE

Many networkers just bumble along in the business and never reach their potential. They think it's because of the prospects they didn't convince. But that's not true – it's because of the prospects they didn't see.

Continually tell your story. If you only obeyed these first three rules, you'd become an outrageous success!

RULE # 4 USE THE LAW OF AVERAGES

The Law of Averages governs the success of every activity in life. It means that if you do the same thing the same way over and over again, under the same circumstances, it will produce a set of results that will always remain constant.

For example, the average payout for a $1 poker machine is around 10:1. For every 10 times you press the button you will receive a collective win of between 60 cents and $20. Your chance of having a win of $20 to $100 is 118:1. There is virtually no skill involved; the machines are programmed to pay out on averages or percentages.

In the insurance business I discovered an average of 1:56. This meant that if I went into the streets and asked a negative question like – "You don't want to buy any life insurance, do you?" – one person in 56 answered 'yes'! This meant that if I asked this question 168 times a day, I'd make 3 sales a day and be in the top 5% of salespeople!

If you stood on a street corner and said to everyone who walked past, "How about joining me in a networking business?" the Law of Averages would give you a result. Perhaps 1:100 would reply 'yes'. The Law of Averages always works.

When I was a kid selling household sponges door-to-door for 20 cents each, my averages were:

$$10 : 7 : 4 : 2$$

For every 10 doors I knocked on between 4pm and 6pm, 7 residents would answer the door. Four residents would listen to my presentation and two would buy a sponge, so I'd make 40 cents which was a lot of money in 1962, especially to an eleven-year-old. I could comfortably knock on 30 doors in an hour, so in a two-hour period I'd make 12 sales, which equalled $2.40. Because I understood how averages worked, I never worried about the 3 doors that never opened, the 3 people who didn't want to hear my presentation, or the 2 people who didn't buy. All I knew was that if I knocked on 10 doors, I'd make 40 cents. This meant that every time my hand touched a door, I'd earn 4 cents regardless of what happened next.

This was a powerful motivating force for me – knock on any 10 doors and I'd make 40 cents! Success was now all just a matter of how quickly I could knock on those doors.

RECORD YOUR RATIOS

Keeping a record of the averages and statistics of my selling activity was a powerful motivator. Soon I didn't care if a door didn't open, if someone wouldn't listen or didn't buy. As long as I knocked on lots of doors and attempted a presentation, I was a success. So now I could relax and have fun knocking on the doors.

> *Recording averages and statistics keeps you positive and on track.*

This is the key to sustained motivation and handling of rejection. When your focus is on your averages, the rest doesn't bother you. You're motivated to make the next call as soon as possible. Without an understanding of averages you will be motivated by *what happens to you next*. If someone says 'No', you might become despondent. If a door doesn't open, you could feel depressed. When you accept and understand the Law of Averages, none of that matters. By keeping the statistics of your calls/presentations/new members, you will quickly develop your own set of averages.

My Personal $9 Poker Machine

When I was a teenager, I had an evening job selling pots, pans, bed linen and blankets, mainly by referral. My ratios were:

$$5 : 3 : 2 : 1$$

For every 5 prospects I called on the telephone, 3 would give me an appointment. I got the chance to present to only two of these prospects because the third either stood me up, cancelled the appointment, wouldn't listen or had some other objection that was beyond my control. Of the 2 who listened, one would buy and I'd make $45. So for every 5 people I called on the phone, I'd end up with $45 commission, which equalled $9 per phone call made.

This meant that every 'yes' on the telephone equated to $15 earned, regardless of whether they did or didn't buy and whether they showed up or not. And regardless of what they said to me! Wow! This was fantastic!

I drew up a big sign with $9 written on it and placed it beside my telephone. For every person who answered the phone I earned $9. For everyone who said 'yes' to a request for an appointment, I'd end up with $15. This meant I was completely in control of my own destiny! Most other salespeople were feeling depressed about a prospect who had said 'no'. Soon I was the number one salesman nationally in the company.

My averages of 5:3:2:1 translated into –

Phone calls	$ 9.00
Appointments	$ 15.00
Presentations	$22.50
Sales	$45.00

I never looked for people who might buy from me. My main goal was to make the phone calls to prospects.

This is the key. Don't go looking for new distributors - look for prospects who will listen to your presentation. The Law of Averages will look after you.

HITTING THE BIG TIME

At age 20 I joined the life insurance business as a salesman. At 21 I was the youngest person ever to sell over one million dollars of insurance in their first year and qualify for the Million Dollar Round Table Club. My averages were:

10 : 5 : 4 : 3 : 1

For every 10 prospects who would answer the phone, 5 would agree to an appointment, one wouldn't keep the appointment, so I would only see 4. Of these 4, I could only complete my presentation to 3, one would buy and I'd make

$300. My focus was always to get 5 people to say 'yes' to an appointment. I never focussed on the prospects who didn't turn up for the interview; or those who wouldn't listen to my presentation or the 2 who didn't buy. These events were just a necessary part of finding the buyer. In fact, if a prospect didn't turn up for an interview, I didn't mind because I'd planned for one to stand me up, so when it happened, I'd still earned $60.

> *You are in the numbers business.*

I knew that if 10 people answered the phone, 5 would agree to see me and I'd end up with $300 commission. This equalled $30 for every time a prospect answered the phone.

My average of 10:5:4:3:1 translated into –

Phone calls	$ 30.00
Appointments	$ 60.00
Presentations	$ 75.00
Closes	$100.00
Sales	$300.00

By age 21, I owned my own home, drove a late model Mercedes-Benz and was living a very comfortable lifestyle. It was now simply a matter of how often I could get groups of 5 prospects to say 'yes' to an appointment over the telephone.

RULE #5 IMPROVE YOUR AVERAGES

In the insurance business, I knew that every time I picked up the phone and spoke to someone – anyone – I'd earn

$30. However, my ratio of 10 phone calls to 5 appointments wasn't good enough in my opinion, because it meant that I was burning up too many prospects. I needed an appointment-getting system that could produce at least 8 appointments from 10 calls. This meant that I wouldn't have to prospect as hard as I had been because I didn't use them up so fast on the phone. My appointment-to-presentation ratio of 5:4 meant that 20% of my prospects weren't turning up so I could close this gap if I phoned *better-qualified* prospects. My presentations-to-close average of 3:1 could also be improved. But I still knew that **even if I didn't change a thing** I'd still make $30 each time I picked up the telephone.

> *The Law of Averages*
> *will always work for you.*

Keeping ratios keeps you sane, tells you where you need improvement and shows you how successful you can be. It lets you focus on the activities that get results, not on what happens to you next.

AVERAGES IN A NETWORKING BUSINESS

I've been training Network Marketers since the seventies and have collected the results of individuals and organisations that have achieved the top levels of success.

A typical average in network marketing is

10 : 6 : 3 : 1

Of every ten prospects who listen to your presentation, 6 get excited about it and say they'll start in the business. Half of these actually get started and one of these 3 becomes successful, one fades into obscurity and other continues to buy the products. So every 10 times you show the plan you end up with one productive long-term distributor.

Now for the big question:

> *How long does it take you to talk*
> *to 10 people about the business?*

Your answer to this question will determine your growth rate. In the life insurance business, everyone sold a million dollars worth of insurance – it just took some people a lot longer to do it than others. Some took 3-5 years to do it while others did it in one year – and that's where the prizes and awards lay. I became so organised in seeing people that I could sell a million every 12 weeks! So it was a **planning problem** - not a selling problem! Network Marketing is exactly the same. The reason so many Network Marketers fail to achieve lofty levels of success is not because of the prospects they didn't convince -it's because of the prospects they **didn't see!** If you want to double your results immediately, here's the answer-

> *See next year's prospects this year.*

Next year you'll be calling on new prospects to tell them about the business, right? Well, call them **early!** See them **this** year - go and see them **now!** You don't have a selling problem. The key is to be highly organised and motivated to talk to as many people as you can. See **everyone** as soon as possible! **Big time** success in Networking is not about convincing people – it's about being organised and disciplined to see as many people as you can – and as soon as possible. Improving your averages is only a learning process.

Section 2

How To
Get To
'Yes'

The Four Keys Technique

When you talk about the business, do your prospects believe you?

The short answer is – **no**. They expect you to try to convince them to make a commitment. They are waiting for you to start selling so they are likely to be guarded or defensive - regardless of how well you know them. Here's the problem you face-

> *Prospects will raise objections*
> *to anything you say.*

Not because of the validity of what you said but because **you** said it. If you say it, it's your idea, not theirs, so prospects feel justified in raising objections. On the other hand –

> *Everything your prospects tell you is true.*

This is because if they say it, it's **their** idea, not yours. This makes the idea acceptable and they feel no urge to raise objections about it.

The technique you are about to discover will enable you to get your prospects to tell you what they really want while **you** do the listening.

When you say to a prospect, "You will be able to live a lifestyle that gives you everything you want", he might respond, "But I'm not unhappy with the way I live now." Chances are that the objection is not even true. He only raised the objection because **you** made a statement.

But if your prospect says *exactly the same thing* to you, it would be true. For example if your prospect says, "I'd like to improve my lifestyle and have more of the good things in life," there would be no objection raised because he said it. It was his idea, not yours.

> *When you use the 'Four Keys' Technique*
> *your prospects will tell you what they*
> *really want while you do the listening.*

WHY PEOPLE OBJECT

I once asked a networker how he had fared with a prospect in a recent presentation. He replied, "Not very well – she wasn't very interested." I asked him what he meant and he repeated, "I don't know really - she just wasn't interested."

> *There are no uninterested prospects,*
> *only uninteresting presentations.*

What he really meant was that he, the networker, was not very interesting.

You see, when you're interesting, your prospects will be interested.

THE FOUR KEYS TO THE TREASURE CHEST OF NETWORK MARKETING

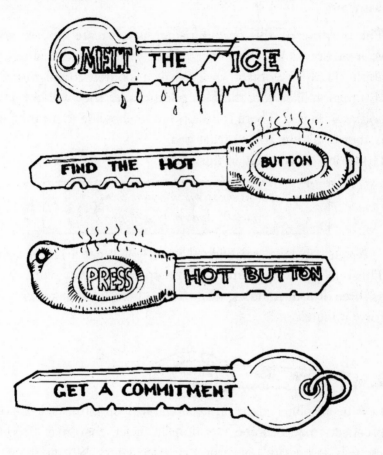

These four keys are the combination for getting from a cold start to a 'yes' in the shortest possible time.

1.

The purpose of this opening stage is to create rapport with your prospects by telling them about yourself and finding out about them. The objective of this key is purely to sell yourself. If a person likes you, there's a good chance they will like what comes with you. There is little point in showing them the plan if they don't like you or trust you.

How long do you stay in this stage?

> *For as long as it takes you to sell yourself and establish trust.*

When you have established trust, you'll get a fair hearing. This is all you want. With some prospects, this can take as little as three or four minutes, while with others, it can take thirty or forty minutes.

2.

Let's be absolutely clear on what will happen in this stage. Your prospects may become emotionally upset; they may become excited, depressed, concerned or even angry. Not angry with you, but with themselves. **There's no room for complacency in this part of the presentation!** When people are complacent about their goals or ambitions, they'll be complacent in their work habits. You don't need complacent people in your network. People who have strong emotional reasons for joining will be motivated to make it work. In this stage, you will learn how to discover the person's **Primary Motivating Factor or PMF**.

Their **PMF** is the reason they will want to join your business.

> *Everyone is motivated by one of two things:*
> *To make a gain*
> *or*
> *avoid a pain.*

With this key, you'll see how to uncover their Primary Motivating Factor and how to light a fire under them once you've found it. This is where your prospects tell you what gains they want to make and what pains they want to avoid. This is the most important of the Four Keys, because your prospects will be verbalising their hopes, dreams and fears.

WHY PEOPLE BUY

Our research has shown that most peoples' Primary Motivating Factors for joining a Network Marketing organisation are:

Extra income
Financial freedom
Have own business
More spare time
Personal development
Helping others
Meeting new people
Retirement
Leave a legacy

When you study this list, you'll notice that one of the reasons listed was **your** primary reason for wanting to have a Network Marketing business. There are probably some secondary reasons too, but one reason always takes precedence over the others. This is your Primary Motivating Factor.

While the Primary Motivating Factor is of absolute importance, it's critical to understand that

> *Not everyone's Primary Motivating Factor for joining Network Marketing is the same as yours.*

For example, you might love chocolate ice cream. This doesn't mean that everyone does. Some people prefer strawberry or caramel. But if you love chocolate, not only will you find it easy to talk about it, but you'll also want to share it with everyone, and you would find it difficult to understand why everyone didn't like it. Most people do like chocolate ice cream, but it is not necessarily everybody's number one choice. Some people are even allergic to it.

The following are **true-life stories** which show the power of the Primary Motivating Factor.

WHY RON DIDN'T JOIN

Albert was a distributor. He joined Network Marketing because he wanted financial freedom. He wanted to be his own boss and determine his own income. He wanted the freedom to come and go as he pleased, to send his kids to the best schools, to have a holiday home, and so on. Financial freedom was his Primary Motivating Factor because it could give him all these things. He was emotionally involved in his goals and could talk about them with endless, sincere enthusiasm.

At a local fundraising event, he met a potential recruit named Ron and invited him to look at the business. Albert showed Ron the plan with his usual great enthusiasm. Ron was impressed. He said he'd join up.

In fact, Albert never saw Ron again, and was left in a state of confusion about what had happened. Why didn't Ron start?

The problem was Ron's Primary Motivating Factor was not financial freedom. He did not have an ambition to be rich, live in a big home and drive a fancy car. He was happy with the modest home he had inherited from his mother. He preferred to catch the train and read the paper, rather than be stuck in the road traffic. Ron felt that financial freedom was OK, but it was not enough to motivate him to make a commitment.

What *really* motivated Ron was the opportunity to meet new people, to learn new skills and contribute to his community – that's why he was involved in fundraising. But he never had the opportunity to talk about those things, because Albert was busy shovelling **financial freedom** down his throat. Ron had certainly been swept along with Albert's enthusiastic presentation, but when the sun rose the next day, he'd cooled off. Within a couple of days, Ron had virtually forgotten about Albert's highly enthusiastic presentation. Ron's Primary Motivating Factor of **helping others** had not been uncovered.

Jan's Misjudgement

Jan was a thirty-four-year-old solo mother with two children. She had been in Network Marketing for two years. She met David at a dinner party. David seemed interested in her

Networking activities and encouraged her to tell him more. Jan's own Primary Motivating Factor was to have enough time to raise and educate her two children, but she was perceptive enough to know that this was not everyone's number one priority.

David was in his fifties and was a self-employed contract cleaner, so Jan assumed that retirement would be high on his list of priorities. When she talked about the business, her conversation centred heavily on its effectiveness in affording people a comfortable retirement.

She was devastated at the end of the evening when David told her that he never wanted to retire – he saw it as an early death. Jan had wrongly assumed that retirement would be David's Primary Motivating Factor. Consequently, he never felt motivated to join her.

> *Never Assume.*
> *It can make an*
> *ASS out of U and ME.*

When you assume another person's Primary Motivating Factor, you're likely to get it wrong. Even if your assumption is correct, it will seem like your idea, and not your prospect's idea, so it won't have the same impact and motivational power.

How to Uncover the Primary Motivating Factor

You will need a visual aid with the Primary Motivating Factors listed. This list can be on the back of your business card, in a prepared visual aid or on a pocket-sized card. Here's the list again:

> Extra income
> Financial freedom
> Have own business
> More spare time
> Personal development
> Helping others
> Meeting new people
> Retirement
> Leave a legacy.

Here's a simple technique for producing your list –
Ask your prospect this question –

**"Do you know why people start
a networking business?"**

The beauty of this simple question is that 'No' gives you
permission to say,

"Let me show you."

At this point, produce your list.

If your prospect answers, 'Yes' to your question, you ask,

"Why do they join?"

Your prospect will give you some real or half-baked reasons
about why he thinks people start a Network Marketing
business. When he runs out of reasons, ask, "Anything else?"
He replies, "No," so you say,

"Let me show you,"

and produce your list of Primary Motivating Factors.

Next, ask the **Five Solid Gold Questions.**

These questions will be the five most valuable questions you
will ever ask. They will give you an express ride to Network

Marketing stardom (if that's your Primary Motivating Factor). Learn these questions and make them part of you. The order must **not** be changed. This is the part you promised you would learn.

Here Are the Five Solid Gold Questions.

1. What is your number one priority?
2. Why did you pick that one?
3. Why is that important to you?
4. What are the consequences of not having that opportunity?
5. Why would that worry you?

Learn these questions, word for word. Don't get sidetracked when you ask them. It is critical that they are kept in order.

Some networkers prefer to use the 'curiosity approach' when they talk to new prospects while others prefer the 'direct approach'. In the following examples, the approach used tends to be more direct because it's simpler to demonstrate. The transcripts are of real interviews.

ANGIE MEETS RAY AND RUTH

Ray and Ruth were a couple in their mid twenties who had just moved into their new home two doors down from Angie. In the course of neighbourly conversation, Angie mentioned that she was involved in a marketing business and would be happy to give them the opportunity of seeing how it worked.

Ruth said that she didn't think they'd be interested because they didn't have much time available. Ray worked two jobs, and she said that at night her hands were full settling into the new home.

Angie said that she found that this was the case with most people who had two jobs and were just moving into a new home, but she would be happy to show them anyway, as they may be interested some time in the future. Angie invited them to 'drop by' her home for a coffee. "Would Saturday afternoon around four be O.K.?" she asked. Ray and Ruth agreed. They arrived at four o'clock and after a chat and coffee, Angie told them that it was a networking business. Ray and Ruth told Angie they had heard about networking, knew people who had tried it and failed, thought it had something to do with soap, and asked, "Is it like Amway?" Here's how Angie handled it:

ANGIE: "Do you know why people start a networking business?"

RAY: "That's a bit like pyramid selling, isn't it?"

ANGIE: "Let me show you."

ANGIE: (Casually producing her **PMF** card) "These are the main reasons people start in Network Marketing **What would be your number one priority?**"

RAY: "Aaahhh... ummm... For us, it would have to be financial freedom."

RUTH: (Firmly) "That's for sure!"

ANGIE: **"Why did you pick that one?"**

RAY: "Because I work two jobs to pay the mortgage and Ruth works overtime so that when we decide to start a family, we'll have a nest egg to fall back on. We want our kids to have a good education and we don't want to always be scratching for money."

ANGIE: **"Why is that important to you?"**

RAY: "As I said, we want to get the house paid off and give our kids a good education. Ruth and I never had those opportunities."

RUTH: (Taking over) "That's right. My parents always struggled to make ends meet. We don't want our lives to be like that."

ANGIE: **"What would be the consequences of not having financial freedom?"**

RAY: "We'd be in the same boat as our parents. It would mean strict budgeting and rarely making ends meet."

RUTH: "It costs a lot to give your kids a good education. Without extra money, we wouldn't be able to give them that headstart in life."

ANGIE: **"Why would that worry you?"**

RAY: (Sounding tense) "Like we said, if you don't try to achieve financial freedom, it will only ever be a struggle, and who wants that?"

RUTH: "Plus we'll need to plan for retirement. That's why we work so hard now."

Analysis:

Nothing was said in this conversation that wouldn't be said with any similar couple. The difference, however, is that in this conversation Angie used the Five Solid Gold Questions and Ruth and Ray disclosed their Primary Motivating Factors. Even if Angie had been lucky enough to pick financial freedom as their **PMF**, Ray and Ruth would have thought it was her idea, not theirs. If Angie had talked about financial freedom, Ruth and Ray would probably have raised objections because Angie said it. But because **they** had said it, it was real – there could be no objections.

Let's consider these five questions:

1. *"What is your number one priority?"*

The real question was, "Why would you join my Network Marketing business today?" Ray said their Primary Motivating Factor was **financial freedom**. That's why they would both join.

2. *"Why did you pick that one?"*

This question really asks, "Why would you join for that reason?" They both explained that they wanted to pay off their house, give their kids a good education and never be short of money.

3. *"Why is that important to you?"*

This question asks, "Tell me again - why would you join for that reason?" Ray said, "As I said ..." and repeated himself, reinforcing the reasons why they should join the business. Ruth also joined in with more reasons why financial freedom was the number one reason they should join. After all, her parents had difficulty in making ends meet and she didn't want to live in similar circumstances.

4. *"What would be the consequences of not having financial freedom?"*

This question really asks, "What will happen to you if you don't join?" Now they both became excited. They told Angie they didn't want to end up like their parents and they didn't want their kids to miss out on a good education because there wasn't enough money.

5. *"Why would that worry you?"*

This question asked them to repeat their number one priority. They both became animated. They emphasised again and again why **financial freedom** was the number one reason they would join the business today.

They told Angie. She *didn't* tell them.

If Angie had said exactly the same things to them, they would probably have given her reasons why they couldn't proceed, but since they told her why they would join, the reasons were real.

After this interview, Angie showed them how the plan worked and replayed their words to them to describe the benefits and outcomes the business could provide. She showed the gains they would make and the pains they'd avoid. From Ray and Ruth's standpoint, it was the perfect answer to their dreams because they were hearing their words, their goals and fears being addressed in a proposed business plan. It was all theirs, not Angie's.

How Bruno cracked a tough nut

Bruno was an engineer who worked on an Association Committee with other engineers, including Jim. Bruno had started a network marketing business a year earlier and saw it as a way of getting out of what he felt was the day to day routine of engineering. He was looking at broader horizons.

Bruno had mentioned a 'business opportunity' to Jim on several occasions but had only received a cold response. Jim's sister had been in 'one of those schemes' and had tried to get him to join, but he had resisted because he felt he was an engineer, not a salesman, and he didn't want to 'pester his friends'.

Over coffee one evening, Bruno casually produced his new business card which had the list of Primary Motivating Factors printed on the back. Jim looked at the card, which had the words 'Networking and Distribution' printed under Bruno's name.

BRUNO: "Do you know what networking is about, Jim?"

JIM: "Yeah, like I said, my sister was in it. It's one of those pyramid schemes, isn't it?"

BRUNO: "Well, let me show you."

Bruno turned the business card over to reveal the list of Primary Motivating Factors.

BRUNO: "What would be your number one priority on this list, Jim?"

JIM: "Aaah... I suppose, having my own business and helping others."

BRUNO: "Why did you pick those two?"

JIM: "I'd like the chance of working for myself because I've been running on the engineering treadmill for nearly twenty years. If I ever did it, though, I'd like to be able to help others in the process. I get a buzz out of doing that. That's why I volunteered for this Committee."

BRUNO: "Why is that important to you?"

JIM: "As I said, the future only holds more of the same old grind for me - you know what it's like, Bruno - I'm beginning to think more and more about my retirement, and that's sad. I'd like to do something else, but at age thirty eight, it's too big a risk to take."

BRUNO: "Well, what are the consequences of not having your own business?"

JIM: (Becoming uneasy) "Like I said, it would be more of the same old grind. Guys our age die from stress, you know. If I had more time, I could join the Parents Committee at my son's school; I could spend more time in my workshop and call my own shots. I'm tired of others controlling my life."

BRUNO: "Why does all that worry you?"

JIM: "Because if I had my time over Bruno, I'd do things differently. I'd do more living and less working. I want to do things for myself for a change."

BRUNO: "That's exactly what the Networking business is designed to let you do. It gives you more time, more freedom, and the advantages of being in your own business, while letting you help others, without the risk of starting a new career. Let me show you how it worked for me."

For over a year, Bruno had tried to get Jim interested in the business, without success. When Bruno learned the secret of the **Five Solid Gold Questions,** he realised that for over a year he had been trying to tell Jim what he should do with his life. It had all been Bruno's idea, not Jim's. The list on the back of Bruno's card and the **Five Solid Gold Questions** allowed Jim to talk about why he would join the business.

When Jim saw the business plan, he couldn't believe his eyes. "Why hasn't anyone ever shown me this before?" he demanded. The answer was that he'd only ever been **told** why he should join – nobody had ever asked him to talk about his Primary Motivating Factors.

HOW THE DENTIST GOT DRILLED

This is an event that happened to me. Frank, aged 44, was my dentist; he owned a million dollar home on the beach, a luxury car and was always busy. By most people's standards, he was very successful. One day I was at the local shopping centre when I saw him sitting in a cafe. I joined him for coffee.

ALLAN: "How's business Frank?"

FRANK: (unenthusiastic) "OK..."

ALLAN: (Humorously) "Come on Frank, you live on the beach, you've got plenty of work and make a lot of money – that's got to be good."

FRANK: "It's a living, I suppose."

ALLAN: "Well, if you don't like it Frank, why not quit and do something else?"

FRANK: "I doubt I'll be doing that Allan."

ALLAN: "Why not?"

FRANK: (In a matter of fact tone) "Because I'm a dentist, I've always been a dentist – that's what I do."

ALLAN: (Interested) "Hmmm... when did you decide to become a dentist Frank?"

FRANK: "When I was 18 and at University. I didn't make medicine. Dentistry was my next option."

ALLAN: "Do you like being a dentist, Frank?"

FRANK: (offhandedly) "Not really, but it pays the bills."

ALLAN: "Frank, if an 18-year-old student walked into your surgery and told you what to do with your life for the next 20 years, would you listen to him?"

FRANK: (laughing) "There's not much an 18-year-old can tell a 44-year-old about life."

ALLAN: "So you wouldn't listen to him?"
FRANK: "No way!"
ALLAN: "Then, why are you...?"

The conversation came to a dead stop. Frank was dumbstruck. You see, he had never considered how the spur-of-the-moment decision of an 18 year-old university student was controlling the direction of his life at age 44. I could see the impact this question was having on him and this was an opportunity too good to miss. I reached into my pocket and pulled out my business card with the PMF list printed on the back. I placed it in front of him.

ALLAN: "Frank, look at this list. What would you say is your number one priority in life?"

After what seemed an endless silence he finally answered.

FRANK: "More spare time."
ALLAN: "Why did you choose that one?"
FRANK: "I get up at six o'clock every morning to get ready for my first patient at 8:30am. I work until 6pm and my day is full of complaining people who aren't happy to see me. I never have time for myself or my kids, even on the weekends. I'm too worn out to do anything worthwhile. Free time is something I've never really had."
ALLAN: "Why is that important to you, Frank?"
FRANK: (Becoming uneasy) "As I said, my life is a minute-by-minute schedule. I think I'd rather be a school teacher so I could have more time and plenty of holidays."

ALLAN: "Meaning?"

FRANK: "Dentistry is not what it may seem. When I first decided to do it..."

Frank spoke passionately for almost 5 minutes about the prison in which he felt dentistry had trapped him.

ALLAN: "What are the consequences of not having the opportunity of more time Frank?"

FRANK: (Sounding desperate) "I'd spend the rest of my life chained to the surgery. My kids are growing up fast and they're not getting much quality time from me. My wife says she has had enough of the stressed condition I always seem to be in."

Frank's face was becoming pale. His eyes were watery. I thought he was about to burst into tears. For the first time in 20 years he was verbalising all the things that had been going around his head.

ALLAN: (Gently) "Why does all that worry you Frank?"

Frank didn't answer. He couldn't. It worried him alright. He just sat there, silent. I didn't press for more information because I didn't think he could take it. Besides, I was supposed to be buying cornflakes, not changing Frank's life.

Three months later I went to see Frank at his surgery. His receptionist told me that he was gone. He had come in one Monday, announced that a friend was taking over the practice and he was having time off. No one had seen him for almost three months. A year later I heard that he was in America selling motels on commission and having a great time. I still don't know where Frank is now or what he's doing, but what happened here

33

is important because it shows how powerful this technique can be and how it can change the lives of people you least expect.

Maybe Frank has a Network Marketing business some-where....

THE PROSPECT WITHOUT A PRIORITY

Occasionally you'll meet a prospect who claims he doesn't have a priority.

Some people claim not to have a number one priority for one of two reasons.

First, they genuinely don't have a number one priority, or number two or number three priorities either. In this case, thank them for their time and look for another prospect. Don't waste your time with people who do not have hopes, dreams and priorities. Second, they are afraid to choose a priority in case they are obliged to act on it.

Here's how to handle these prospects:

YOU: "What is your number one priority?"

PROSPECT: "None of those really..."

YOU: "None?"

PROSPECT. "No, none are important to me right now."

YOU: (casually) "Well, if one **was** to be important which one would it be?"

PROSPECT. "Well, if one was important... it would probably be **financial freedom."**

YOU: "Why that one?"

PROSPECT. "Because it's important to have money and..."

Now you continue with the **Five Solid Gold Questions.**

The Power of Silence

After you ask a question, you must remain completely silent until the prospect completes an answer. Resist all temptation to help them select their priority, *it must be their idea, not yours.* They need to tell you why they need to join your business. This is probably the first time in the prospect's life that someone has asked such important questions and given him the time to express his own answers. Even if your prospect has been approached several times previously about Network Marketing, it's probably the first time someone has asked questions and then shut up. Your prospect's answers will also indicate the level of commitment he is likely to make in the business over the long term.

How to Separate the Sheep from the Goats

The sincerity and depth of the prospects' answers to the **Five Solid Gold Questions** will reveal how motivated they could be in the business. If their answers are off-handed, casual or not convincing, then you need to think carefully about whether or not you should be inviting them to join your network. Unless your prospects have a fire in the belly they won't do much more than complain. If their answers to the **Five Solid Gold Questions** are weak, you're better off to look for another prospect. Prospects who give weak responses will be leaners and constantly take up your time. The prospects with priorities and dreams will succeed, even in spite of you.

> *Prospects with priorities will always succeed.*
> *You can only help speed up this process.*

Building a Network Marketing business is like planting a garden. You till the soil, fertilise it, keep the weeds out and make sure it is protected from bad weather. But some seeds will grow while others will wither. All you can do is water, fertilise and weed. The strong seeds will grow regardless of you.

If the seeds you plant are weak you will be forever propping them up and hoping they will grow. Don't fool yourself into believing a weak seed can be encouraged to grow into a strong and beautiful plant. That rarely happens. The real secret is to plant the strong seeds. This is the purpose of the **Five Solid Gold Questions** – they will test the potential strength of the seed before you plant it.

If a prospect is not strong with his answers to the questions, he could be the wrong prospect. Perhaps the timing is wrong for him. Or he may simply become a purchaser of the products. Sponsor as many prospects as possible but spend most of your time with the strong seeds.

USING THE LIST WITH A GROUP

With a little practice, you will find this step an amazing way to make a presentation to a group of prospects. You can either use a prepared PMF list or you can ask the audience to call out the reasons why people would join a Network Marketing group. With a prepared list you ask someone, "What is your number one priority?" and you're away! Then repeat the process for a second and third prospect and very quickly you'll have the entire audience telling you why they want to join the business.

If you prefer to write the list by hand during your presentation, ask each person who volunteered a priority, "Why did you choose that one?" and follow through with all the questions. It's great fun to have the entire group telling each other why it's important to join – and you never have to make a statement! All you have to do is nod your head and give encouragement.

3.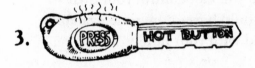

SHOWING THE PLAN

This is where most Network Marketers shine. This is where you demonstrate how your plan is the solution to the hopes, fears and dreams that were uncovered in the second key. **Find the Hot Button.** Your upline will have shown you a system of presenting the business plan that is proven and gets results.

It's critical, however, that you understand the next statement –

> *The business plan is only a*
> *solution to a problem, or*
> *the way to realise a dream.*

A solution should make logical sense. But logic only opens the mind. The **Five Solid Gold Questions** unlock the emotions and motivate the right prospects to want to find their own solution. When you show only solutions without having first uncovered a person's Primary Motivating Factor, the prospect is likely to be swept up in the enthusiasm of it all but not be emotionally motivated. That's why prospects often go cold within a few days.

When you show the plan, use your prospect's own words in the plan.

For example –

> **"So this means you can control your own
> destiny and you would have more time available
> to spend with your family"**
>
> or
>
> **"This means you can retire in the style and
> comfort you said you wanted."**

When you repeat your prospect's words as you show the business plan, it becomes personal to them. It becomes meaningful and motivational. It's **their** ideas and words, not yours.

4.  GET A COMMITMENT

When you use these techniques exactly as presented, asking your prospect to join you is not a dramatic event. They should be so fired up with their own enthusiasm that getting started in the business is the obvious course of action. Always approach your presentations with the attitude that getting started is the perfectly natural thing to do. Your style should be businesslike but relaxed, as though you do it every day.

The important thing to remember is that when the time is right for your prospects to join the business *you must ask them to join*.

Be clear, confident and definite and tell them that you want them to join. Today – not tomorrow.

WHY THIS SYSTEM WORKS

The **Four Keys** system is a proven way for getting to 'yes' so you must stick to the formula to achieve maximum results. Most Network Marketers that I have met are good in the **Melt the Ice** stage. They've learned how to talk with others in a friendly way and build rapport. Most however, do not have an effective '**Find the Hot Button**' stage – they go straight from '**Melt the Ice**' to '**Press the Hot Button**'. Even if their presentation of the business plan is an excellent one, the prospects are not necessarily motivated to action because they are not emotionally disturbed.

This is the main reason why so many prospects can become excited by your presentation of the plan but have completely cooled off a day or two later. Some networkers get so carried away with showing the plan that they can sell the idea but then keep talking so much that they buy it back!

The business plan is *only the solution* to pains your prospects want to avoid or to gains they want to make. There is no point in showing the plan until you have uncovered a prospect's Primary Motivating Factor and have him fired up about it.

If you are great at **Finding Hot Buttons** there's no need to be overly concerned about **Getting a Commitment**. When you know how to get prospects emotionally disturbed, they will start looking for their own solutions to their problems.

Find Hot Buttons and press them and building your network will be simple.

Section 3

Six Strategic Skills For Powerful Presenting

Here are six subtle, but dramatically effective skills that will put potency into your presentations.

SKILL #1 – BRIDGING

Bridging is a technique that keeps the conversation moving and avoids the situation where you might talk too much or your prospect talks too little.

It's frustrating to think of a brilliant open-ended question and to receive a short answer in reply.

True Life Story:

How Sue warmed up a cold fish

Here's an example of Sue, the distributor, trying to build rapport with her prospect, Fred. Fred worked for a computer company and agreed to give Sue a hearing during his lunch break. Fred seemed a little abrupt at first and didn't sound like the conversational type, which Sue found a little daunting.

SUE: "How did you happen to get into this business, Fred?"

FRED: "I've always been interested in computers."

At this point Sue doesn't have much information to work with, so she's forced to ask another open-ended question.

SUE: "What do you like most about the computer business?"

FRED: "It's always changing."

Again, a short answer forces her to think of another open-ended question in an attempt to pry open this hard-nosed clam. The problem is, even if she kept asking good open-ended questions, after a while the conversation would begin to sound like an interrogation with Sue as the Chief of Police.

Prospects who give short answers can be best handled with 'bridges' to keep them talking. Powerful bridges include-

Meaning...?
For example?
So then...?
Therefore...?
Then you...?
Which means...?

Each bridge must be followed by silence on your part. Fortunately, Sue had learned how to use bridges and this is how her conversation with Fred really went-

SUE:	"How did you happen to get into this business, Fred?"
FRED:	"I've always been interested in computers."
SUE:	"Meannninnng ...?"
FRED:	"Meaning the installation of network systems into large and medium-sized business."
SUE:	"Which means ...?"
FRED:	"Which means I help improve the overall efficiency of a business by creating software that makes their life easier."
SUE:	"For example ...?"

FRED: "Well, for example, yesterday I installed a system for a company that had serious accounting problems. They called me and..."

In this case, Sue has not only successfully cracked a tough nut, but she doesn't sound like an investigator. And she's not doing most of the talking. She's getting lots of useful information about Fred and he's talking about his number one subject - himself.

When you use a bridge, do these three things –

1. Lean forward, palm out.
2. Stretch the last letter of the bridge.
3. Lean back and shut up.

Using Bridges to keep things moving

Leaning forward with your palm out does two things. First, it non-verbally says that you are non-threatening and second, it tells the listener that it is his turn to talk by 'handing over' the control. Stretching the last letter of the bridge almost converts it into a question, but not stretching it can make it sound like a statement.

For example:

FRED: "... so businesses can operate more efficiently."

SUE: "Which meannnsss ...?" (stretched)

FRED: "Which means people's lives are made easier and they can deal better with their customers. You know, most businesses don't have a good system and..."

By not stretching the last syllable of a bridge, you can make it sound like a statement or opinion. It can even sound affronting.

When you've used a bridge, *shut up!* Resist the urge to put pearls of wisdom into the seemingly endless silence that can sometimes follow the use of a bridge. The open palm shows that the responsibility to speak next has been given to the prospect, so let him come up with the next statement.

THE BODY LANGUAGE OF LISTENING

Here's an example of how bridging can uncover hidden motivations and draw out information from a prospect.

After you have given the control, you lean back with your hand on your chin in the evaluation position. This quickly conditions the listener to continue talking for as long as you are leaning back.

Let's say that your prospect has chosen Financial Freedom as their Number One Priority-

YOU: "What is your Number One Priority?"

PROSPECT: "Financial Freedom."

YOU: "Why did you choose that?"

PROSPECT: "Because it's important that I have the money to do all the things I want to do in life."

YOU: (leaning forward, palm out) "Meaninnnnng ...?"

PROSPECT: "...meaning enough money to give my kids a good education and live in a comfortable manner."

YOU: (leaning forward, palm out) "comfortable Meaninnnnng ...?"

PROSPECT: '...meaning having enough money to go on an extensive vacation, drive a nice car or buy a few little luxuries occasionally."

YOU: "...for example ...?"

PROSPECT: "...well, for example, if I wanted to travel, I'd like to be able to..."

By using the two bridges 'meaning' and 'for example', your prospect is now talking about what he thinks, feels and believes and, and, most important, **you're** not doing all the talking.

Bridges are, in effect, a type of open-ended question. They are best used in presentations with people who don't speak much or who give short answers to questions. When you first use bridges it may feel strange (particularly if you're a habitual talker) because of the silence that sometimes follows the use of a bridge. But if your listener is used to giving short answers he's also used to experiencing periods of silence during conversation so it all seems perfectly normal to him. Bridges are fun to use, they make presentations more interesting and give you the power of silent control.

Skill #2 – The Head Nod Technique

Most people have never considered head nodding as a powerful persuasion tool. Nodding the head is a gesture used in most countries to show agreement. Its origin is body lowering or bowing; that is, "If I bow to you, I am subordinate to your wishes." So it's a shortened bowing movement.

There are two powerful uses of the Head Nod technique. Body Language is an outward reflection of inner feelings. If you feel positive, your head will begin to make the nodding gesture as you speak. If you feel neutral and **intentionally** start nodding your head, you will begin to experience positive feelings. In other words, positive feelings cause the head to nod - and the reverse is also true; nodding the head causes positive feelings.

> *If you feel positive you'll start nodding*
> *your head. If you nod your head*
> *you'll start feeling positive.*

Head nodding is also contagious. If I nod my head at you, you will usually nod too – even if you don't necessarily agree with what I am saying. This is an excellent tool for getting agreement and co-operation. Then finish each sentence with a verbal affirmation such as,

Isn't it?
Wouldn't you?
Isn't that true?
Fair enough?

When the speaker and listener **both** nod their head, the listener experiences positive feelings and this creates a greater likelihood of a positive outcome. The Head Nodding skill can be easily learned and you can make it a permanent part of your Body Language repertoire in under a week.

The second use of the Head Nod is to keep the conversation going. Here's how it's done. When you've asked an open-ended question or used a bridge and the listener gives his answer, nod your head during his answer. When he finishes speaking *continue* to nod your head *another five times* at a rate of about one nod per second. Usually, by the time you have counted four seconds, the listener will begin speaking again and give you more information. And as long as you stay leaning back with your hand on your chin, there is no pressure on you to speak. This way, you won't sound like an interrogator. When you listen, put one hand on your chin and give it light strokes. Studies of these gesture shows that they encourage others to keep talking for longer periods of time.

Male Chin-stroking   *Female Chin-stroking*

Skill #3 – Minimal Encouragers

As the other person speaks, encourage him to keep going by using minimal encouragers. These include:

I see...
Uh-huh...
Really?
Tell me more...

Minimal encouragers can more than double the amount of information the other person gives you.

Minimal encouragers, combined with the Head Nod technique and bridges are the most effective tools you can learn to keep the presentation rolling along.

SKILL #4 – HOW TO KEEP EYE CONTROL

Research shows that of the information relayed to a person's brain in a face-to-face presentation, 87% comes via the eyes, 9% via the ears, and 4% through the other senses.

If, for example, your prospect is looking at your visual presentation as you are speaking, he will absorb as little as 9% of your message if the message is not directly related to what he sees. So if you draw a picture of a house while talking about travel, he may *not* follow your story. If the message *is* related to the visual presentation, he will absorb only 25% to 30% of your message if he is looking at the visual presentation and not directly at you.

To maintain maximum eye control, use a pen to point to your presentation and, at the same time, verbalise what your prospect sees. Next, lift the pen away from the visual aid and hold it midway between his eyes and your eyes, and nod your head as you speak.

Using the pen to maintain eye-contact

Look over the top of your pen at your prospect's eyes and point only at where you are looking. This has the magnetic effect of lifting your prospect's head so that he is looking at your eyes and now he sees and hears what you are saying, achieving maximum impact with your message. Be sure that the palm of your other hand is visible when you are speaking, maintaining a non-threatening atmosphere.

SKILL #5 – MIRRORING

When two people are mentally 'in sync' with each other, their bodies also move into physical synchronisation by adopting similar postures and by using the same gestures. The purpose of this behaviour is to create rapport between the participants and avoid conflict. Non-verbally, this behaviour is saying "I'm the same as you and I agree with you and your attitudes."

Being 'in sync' to bond with another person begins early in the womb when our body functions and heartbeat match the rhythm of our mother. That's why mirroring is a state to which we are naturally inclined.

Mum, Dad and Rover

As a result, we intuitively copy the people with whom we feel rapport. You can see this occur at business meetings or social events with people who are getting on well with each other. It also explains why, after years of living together, people can start to resemble each other. Then they buy a dog that looks like both of them.

MONKEY SEE, MONKEY DO

The two people in the next illustration show a typical example of how mirroring looks. They're standing with identical postures, holding their drinks the same way – probably the same drink – they dress alike and use similar vocabulary. If one puts his hand in his pocket, the other copies. If the other shifts his weight to the opposite leg, his friend does too. For as long as the two agree and a rapport exists, the mirroring will continue.

Mirroring shows that a rapport exists

Mirroring makes others feel 'at ease'. It's a powerful rapport-building tool. Slow motion video research shows it can include simultaneous blinking, nostril-flaring, eyebrow raising and even simultaneous pupil dilation or contraction. This is remarkable because these micro-gestures cannot be consciously imitated.

CREATING GOOD VIBES

Mirroring the other person's body language and speech patterns is a dynamic way to build rapport quickly. When you meet a new person, mirror their seating position, posture, body angle, gestures, expressions and tone of voice. Before long, they'll start to feel that there's something about you they like. They'll probably describe you as 'easy to be with'. This is because they can see themselves reflected in you.

Creating a rapport by mirroring

A word of warning: don't mirror too early in a new encounter. Many people have become aware of mirroring strategies since I wrote the book **Body Language** and over 100 million people have watched the television series and training videos that followed. It's sometimes wiser to wait a few minutes before mirroring.

MIRRORING DIFFERENCES BETWEEN MEN AND WOMEN

Men's and women's brains are programmed differently to express their emotions. Women use more facial expression and men rely more on body movements and gestures.

Typically, a woman will use an average of six facial expressions in a ten-second listening period to reflect and feed back the speaker's emotions. Her face will mirror the emotions being expressed by the speaker. To someone watching, it can look as if the events being discussed are happening to both women.

Here is a typical ten-second sequence of a woman showing she is listening:

Sadness **Surprise** **Anger** *Joy* **Fear** *Desire*

A woman reads the meaning of what is being said through the speaker's voice tone and body language and registers her understanding by reflecting those emotions. This is exactly what a man needs to do to capture a woman's attention and to keep her listening. Most men are daunted by the prospect of using facial feedback while listening, but it pays big dividends for those who become good at it.

Some men say, "She'll think I'm weird!", but research shows that when a man mirrors a woman's emotions she will describe him as more intelligent, interesting and attractive.

Because of the evolutionary need to withhold emotion in public to stave off possible attack, most men look like they're statues when they listen.

Here is the same range of facial expressions used by a typical man in a ten-second listening period:

Sadness Surprise Anger   Joy   Fear   Desire

This is a light-hearted look at the male listening approach, but recognising the truth in the humour gives it edge. The emotionless mask that men put on while listening allows them to feel in control of the situation, but does not mean they don't experience emotions. Brain scans reveal that men feel emotion as strongly as women do, but avoid showing it in public.

The key to mirroring a man's behaviour is in understanding that he uses his body to signal his attitudes – not his face. Most women find it difficult to mirror an expressionless man but it gets results. If you're a woman, it means you need to reduce your facial expressions so that you don't appear overwhelming or intimidating. Most importantly, **don't mirror what you think he might be feeling.** That can be disastrous if you've got it wrong. You may be described as 'dizzy' or 'scatterbrained'.

Women who use a serious face when listening are described by men as more intelligent, astute and sensible.

Skill #6 – Pacing

Intonation, voice inflection and speed of speaking also synchronise during the mirroring process to further establish mutual attitudes and build rapport. This is known as 'pacing' and it can almost seem as if the two people are singing in time. You will often see a speaker beating time with his hands while the listener matches the rhythm with head nods. As a relationship grows over time the mirroring of the main body language positions becomes less as each person begins to anticipate the other's attitudes. Pacing with the other person then becomes the main medium for maintaining rapport.

Never speak at a faster rate than the other person does. Studies reveal that others say they feel 'pressured' when someone speaks faster than they do. A person's speed of speech shows the rate at which their brain can consciously analyse information. Speak at the same rate or slightly slower than the other person and mirror their inflection and intonation. Pacing is critical when making appointments by telephone because the voice is your only medium, so you need to practise.

Six Tremendous Techniques For Making Positive Impressions

Two good ways of making a poor first impression

Y ou'll never get a second chance to make a first impression. You probably heard your grandmother tell you this. But she didn't need sophisticated computer equipment to know that others will form up to 90% of their opinion about you in less than 4 minutes. Or that they will make at least 25 judgements about you including your age, income, education, authority, friendliness and trustworthiness. They'll even decide how much money they'd lend you before they'd insist on a guarantee. There are, fortunately, four areas over which you can have some control. These are your handshake, smile, dress and personal space.

TECHNIQUE #1 – PALM POWER

One of the most powerful, but least noticed of our body language signals is the use of the palm of the hand. When used correctly, palm power invests its user with a degree of authority and silent command.

There are three main palm gestures: the Palm-Up, the Palm-Down and the Palm-Closed-Finger-Pointed position. The differences in power of each position are shown in this example. Let's say that you ask someone to move to another location in the room. We'll assume you use the same tone of voice, the same words and facial expressions and change only the position of your palm.

The **Palm-Up** (Illustration A) is a non-threatening gesture and the person being asked to move will not feel threatened by the request. It's a gesture used since cavemen to show that the person is not holding any weapons.

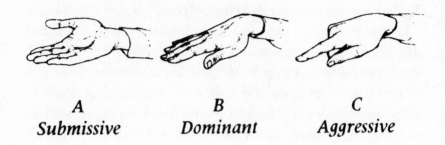

A	*B*	*C*
Submissive	*Dominant*	*Aggressive*

When your palm is turned to face downwards (Illustration B), you communicate immediate authority. The person you have directed will feel that he has been given an order and may feel antagonistic towards you – especially if he doesn't feel you have the right to be so assertive.

If you make a presentation and continually use the **Palm-Down** position you're likely to suffer rejection from your audience.

In Illustration C the pointed finger becomes a symbolic club with which the speaker figuratively beats his listener into submission. The Pointed-Finger is one of the most irritating gestures that a speaker can use, particularly when it beats time with the speaker's words.

Research into both the **Palm-Down** and **Pointed-Finger** gestures show that listeners rate speakers who use these gestures as more aggressive, forceful, smug or arrogant and they can recall less of what the speakers said. This is because the listener was judging the speaker's attitude and not listening to the information.

If you are a habitual finger-pointer, try practicing the **Palm-Up** and **Palm-Down** positions and you'll find that a combination of these positions can create a more relaxed atmosphere and you'll have a more positive effect on your audience.

TECHNIQUE #2 – THE HANDSHAKE

Shaking hands is a relic of the caveman era. Whenever cavemen met, they would hold their arms out with their palms up to show that no weapons were being held or concealed. This Palms-in-Air gesture became modified over the centuries and such gestures as the Single-Palm-Raised, the Palm-Over-Heart and numerous other variations developed. The modem form of this ancient greeting ritual is the interlocking and shaking of the palms which, in most non-Asian countries, is performed both on initial greeting and on departure. The hands are normally pumped three to seven times.

Considering what has already been said about the impact of a command given with the Palm-Up and Palm-Down positions, let's explore the relevance of these two positions in handshaking.

Assume that you have just greeted a new person with a handshake. One of three basic attitudes will be transmitted -

1. Dominance: 'this person is trying to dominate me. I'd better be cautious'.
2. Submission: 'I can dominate this person. He will do what I want.'
3. Equality: 'I like this person. We'll get on well together.'

These attitudes are transmitted unconsciously.

Dominance is communicated when you turn your hand (dark sleeve) so that your palm faces down in the handshake (Illustration 1). Your palm need not be facing the floor directly, but is facing downwards in relation to the other person's palm and this says you want to take the control. Studies of fifty-four successful senior management people revealed not only did forty-two initiate the handshake, but they also used dominant hand shake control. This handshake style is not good for creating rapport, as it is intimidating to most people. It's used mainly by men.

1. Taking the control   *2. Giving the control*

Just as dogs show submission by rolling on their backs and exposing their throat to an aggressor, we humans use the Palm-Up gesture to show submission to others. The reverse of the Dominant Handshake is to offer your hand with your palm facing up (Illustration 2). This is particularly effective when you want to give the other person control or allow him to feel he is in control. It can also say you can be intimidated.

How to create Rapport Through a Handshake

There are two rules for creating rapport in a handshake – first, hold the palms straight - not dominant or submissive, but equal. This makes everyone feel comfortable and is non-threatening.

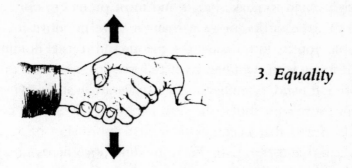

3. Equality

Second, give the same grip pressure that you receive. This can mean that if, for example, you're being introduced to a group of 10 people, you would probably vary the pressure several times and make several adjustments of the angle of the hands.

With this handshake style there are no winners or losers and no one feels intimidated. It makes it easier for everyone to feel open to new ideas and less judgemental of each other.

THE HANDSHAKE TO AVOID

Avoid greeting new people with the Double-Hander. While its objective may be to convey feelings of welcome, warmth and trust, it has the complete opposite effect on the receiver. They perceive the giver to be insincere, less trustworthy or to have ulterior motives. Always stick to the Single-Handed Handshake.

TECHNIQUE #3 – LEFT HAND HOLDING

This strategy may seem obvious at first but few people pay it much attention. Practice holding folders, papers, brief cases, purses and drinks in your left hand. We greet each other using our right hand to shake hands and most of us use our right hand to open doors, move a chair or wave goodbye. If, for example, you are introduced to someone and you are holding a cold drink in your right hand, you're forced to switch the drink to your left hand. Even if you do it successfully and don't spill it over everyone's shoes, the new person receives your cold, wet hand and that becomes their first impression of you – cold, damp and soggy. If you're holding documents in your right hand and you switch hands to open a door, move a chair or respond to a handshake, you might drop the documents and look like a fumbling fool.

Avoid the Double-Hander with new people

TECHNIQUE #4 - SMILE POWER

Humans are the only land animals that draw back the lips to reveal the teeth but do not bite you. Smiling has its origin as an appeasement gesture and is also used by monkeys and chimps to show they are non-threatening.

The smile is an ancient appeasement signal

Our research into this gesture shows that the more frequently you use it, the closer others are likely to stand to you, the more eye contact they will give you, the more likely they will be to touch you and the longer they want to stay with you. In other words, smiling is great for your business and personal life as it shows others you are not a threat to them.

TECHNIQUE #5 – TERRITORIAL RESPECT

We each carry a bubble of space around our body known as Personal Space. Its width depends on population density and what culture the person is from. For example, people raised in most middle-class English-speaking cities have a Personal

Space need of about 46cm (18 inches) and this is why, in non-threatening or social situations, they stand about 1 metre apart (Illustration 1).

1. The Standing distance in most English-speaking Cities

In many parts of Europe, the Mediterranean and South America, the Personal Space need of the locals can be as little as 30cm (12 inches). This means they will be standing too close to most Westerners and may be perceived as 'pushy'.

2. The Standing distance in the Mediterranean

In Illustration 2, if both people were from the Mediterranean region they would probably feel comfortable with each other at this distance. But if one was from London and the other from Rome the Londoner would probably think intimate or aggressive advances were being made. If you are standing close to someone and you notice that they move back each time you move forward, keep your distance and resist moving forward. They're telling you this is the amount of space they need for comfort.

A Touchy Subject

Many non English-speaking cultures are also very tactile or 'touchy' and this further complicates effective communication between cultures. The strategies in these cases are simple – mirror the frequency of touch you receive. If the person isn't touching you, leave them alone. If the person is, for example, Italian or French and seems to be constantly touching you, return their touch or they may think you don't like them.

Technique #6 – Dress for Success

Clothing covers up to 90% of your body and has a powerful effect on other people's perception of your trustworthiness, reliability, expertise, authority, social success and business standing.

While we won't be analysing each component of clothing in this chapter, I will give you the formula for appropriate dress. Women are likely to get it wrong more often than men because women have access to a wider range of styles, colours and designs then men. However, while most men have less choices (and less clothes), most do not have specific locations in the brain to allow them to correctly match patterns and designs and one in eight men is colour blind to red, blue or green.

> *What's the difference between a*
> *single man and a circus clown?*
> *The clown knows when he's*
> *wearing funny clothes.*

The secret to appropriate business dress is in the answer to this question – How does your prospect expect you to be dressed? For you to appear credible, likeable, authoritative, knowledgable, successful and approachable, how would you be dressed in **their** opinion? What suit, shirt, blouse, tie, skirt, shoes, watch, make-up and hairstyle would you be wearing? In **their** opinion – not *yours*.

Remember, your prospect's opinion is the important one here so dress for him or her. This will vary from region to region and dress styles are affected by climate, but there is a standard to which a successful person would be dressed in your region.

"But what about Richard Branson and Bill Gates?" some people ask. "They dress like they just walked out of a wind tunnel!" These people are the exceptions, not the rule. If we all dressed like these people others would find it hard to trust us or follow us. If you lined up the most successful world leaders and business people, you'd notice that there would be a standard to which they would be dressed. And that's the safest standard to follow. Don't handicap yourself by dressing to your own tastes or comfort level. Dress for your prospect's expectations.

> *Dressing like your prospects will make them feel comfortable but they won't necessarily want to follow you.*

Section 5

Body Language-
How To Read
The Signs

*Many people don't see the obvious.
What do you see?*

Almost everyone is now aware that it's possible to read someone's attitude through his or her behaviour. When I wrote **Body Language** in 1976, I had no idea it would have the impact on the world that it has had or that it would sell over 4 million copies in 33 languages.

Our original Body Language research and the countless other studies that have since followed show that, in face-to-face presentations, the impact your message has on your listeners is as follows –

Words   7% – 10% of total impact
Vocal   20% – 30% of total impact
Body Language 60% – 80% of total impact

This shows that the way you look, gesture, smile, dress and move has most of the impact on the other person's attitude toward you. The way you say things is 3 times more important than the words you use.

THE THREE RULES FOR READING

Rule #1. Reading Clusters

Like any language, body language consists of words, sentences, phrases and punctuation. Each gesture is like a single word and may have several different meanings. It is only when you put the word into a sentence with other words that you can fully understand its meaning. Gestures come in sentences called 'clusters'.

Never try to interpret a single gesture in isolation. For example, scratching the head can mean a number of things

- dandruff, fleas, sweating, uncertainty, forgetfulness or lying, depending on the other gestures that occur at the same time. For a correct reading always look for gesture clusters in groups of at least three.

1. A Critical Evaluation cluster

Illustration 1 shows a typical Critical Evaluation cluster – arm across the body, hand to face, thumb supporting the chin, legs crossed and furrowed evebrows.

> *Never try to read a solitary gesture –*
> *It may be just an itchy nose.*

In this section of the book we will be analysing gestures individually but this is not how they normally occur – they come in clusters.

Rule #2. Consider the Context

Gesture clusters should be evaluated in the context in which they occur. If, for example, someone was sitting at a bus terminal with their arms and legs tightly crossed and chin down and it was a cold day, it would most likely mean that he or she was cold, not defensive (Illustration 2).

2. Cold, not defensive

If, however, the person used the same gestures while you were sitting across a table from him trying to sell an idea, the gestures could be correctly interpreted as meaning the person was probably negative or defensive about the situation.

Rule #3. Acknowledge Cultural Differences

A gesture which means one thing in one country can have a dramatically different meaning in another country. For example, the 'ring' gesture shown in Illustration 3 is most commonly recognised in Western countries as meaning 'OK' or 'good'. The 'OK' meaning is now common in all countries which have Western television programs and, although its meaning is fast spreading across the rest of the world, it has other origins and meanings in other places.

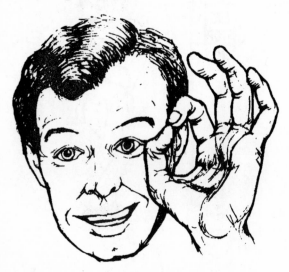

3. 'Good' to the Americans, 'Zero' to the French and an insult to the Greeks

For example, in France it also means 'zero' or 'nothing'; in Japan it means 'money' and in some Mediterranean countries it's a sexual insult.

Most basic body language gestures are the same everywhere. When people are happy they smile; when they are sad or angry they frown or scowl. Nodding the head is almost universally used to indicate 'yes' or affirmation and, as already mentioned, this gesture is a form of head lowering. Smiling is probably inborn as people born with visual impairments also use it even though they may have never actually seen it.

In this chapter I'll present a simple 'dictionary' of body language gestures that are common to most cultures and these are the things you're most likely to see during face-to-face presentations.

WHY WOMEN ARE BETTER RECEIVERS

As reported in our book **Why Men Don't Listen and Women Can't Read Maps,** men's brains are not highly attuned to receiving small non-verbal and vocal cues, which is why many men are often described by women as 'uncaring' or 'insensitive' to other's needs or feelings.

Women at social events everywhere say to men, "Didn't you see the look I was giving you! It should have been obvious to you that I wanted to leave the party!" It would have been obvious to most women, but not to most men.

> *Men are not callous – their brains are*
> *just not programmed to read subtle*
> *body language signals.*

When a woman says she can 'see' someone feels hurt or disagrees with group opinion, she is actually 'seeing' the hurt or disagreement. She's picked up that the person's body language is out of sync with the group opinion and is showing the disagreement. How women can 'see' disagreement, anger, deceit or hurt has always been a source of amazement to most men.

It's because most mens' brains are simply not equipped to read the fine detail of body language like a woman's brain. This is why attempting to lie to a woman in a face-to-face encounter is unwise – a phone call would be safer!

How to Learn to Read Body Language

Set aside fifteen minutes a day to study and read the gestures of other people and to acquire a conscious awareness of your own gestures. A good reading ground is anywhere that people meet and interact. An airport is a particularly good place for observing the entire spectrum of human gestures because people openly express eagerness, anger, sorrow, happiness, impatience and many other emotions through their gestures. Social functions, business meetings and parties are fertile fields for study and watching television also offers an excellent way to learn. Turn down the sound and try to understand what is happening by watching only the picture. By turning the sound up every few minutes, you'll be able to check how accurate your non-verbal readings are and before long it will be possible to watch an entire program without any sound and understand what is happening – just as people who are hearing-impaired do. Use a video camera to film yourself giving a presentation and replay it with the sound off and have your friends and associates evaluate your performance.

An Instant Guide to Body Language

Here's a reference guide to some the most common Body Language signals you are likely to see during your presentation.

ARM CROSSING

Some Observations and Origins –

Crossing the arms in front of the body shows a detached, closed attitude. It's an inborn gesture and 70% of people cross left arm over right. It's almost impossible to re-learn crossing the opposite way. Its purpose appears to be to protect the heart and lungs from attack and most primates also use it for that reason.

This can be a hard nut to crack

Research into this gesture shows that audience members who take this position during a speech can recall 38% less of what is said than those who sit in an open position do. When interviewed about the presenter's performance, the arm-crossers used shorter sentences, gave less eye-contact, sat back more often and were more critical of the presenter's performance than were the arms-uncrossed listeners.

4.   5.   6.

Arm-Crossing can also be seen in several subtle forms including the Half-Arm-Cross (Illustration 4); Holding-Hands-with-Yourself (Illustration 5) which seems to be a relic from when your parent held your hand if you were nervous and Holding-an-Object-with-Both-Hands (Illustration 6). The purpose of holding a purse, glass or folder with two hands is to achieve a sense of security by having the arms in front of the body. Fiddling with a ring, watch or cufflink on the opposite hand achieves the same result. Illustration 7 shows the man on the right using a cluster of gestures in a correct context. He is using the Arms-Crossed position, his legs are spread (male aggression), one eyebrow raised (critical), tight-lipped smile (withholding), and body facing away (disinterested). He is feeling excluded by the other two people who are building a rapport with each other by mirroring.

7. The man on the right feels excluded

THE PROBLEMS OF CAUSE AND EFFECT

Let's say, for example, that a person feels negative, defensive, non-participative or hostile. There is a good chance he will non-verbally signal this by crossing his arms on his chest. We also know from research that in an arms-crossed position a person's retention of what is said diminishes by about 40 per cent and his attitude becomes more critical.

Try this simple experiment. Sit back and tightly cross your arms on your chest. How do you feel? Restrained? Uninvolved? Non-participative? Studies show that if you cross your arms for **any** reason you will begin experiencing the negative effects of this gesture. It's a cause and effect situation. Habitual arm-crossers always claim they feel 'comfortable' because the arm-crossing gesture will feel comfortable when they feel the corresponding emotions. Even if you don't believe that arm crossing is a negative signal, your listener will unconsciously read you as negative or unapproachable. That's why it is hard to convince a group of people in a cold room. The ideal room temperature for presenting should be 21°C.

Some useful strategies

1. Eliminate arm crossing from your repertoire. Your listeners will remember less of what you say, are more critical of your performance and will like you less. Practice open body language.
2. Where possible, give your audience chairs with arms. This allows them to keep their arms uncrossed and want to participate more. Avoid having armless chairs too close together as it encourages participants to cross their arms to avoid touching the person beside them.
3. If your audience sit with their arms crossed you can break the position by asking them to raise their hands to answer questions, give them physical involvement exercises to do, hand out pens and paper for note-taking or serve them hot drinks.

HAND-TO-FACE TOUCHING

Some Observations and Origins

All researchers who have investigated hand-to-face touching agree that it relates to negative emotions. Westerners and most Europeans increase their hand-to-face contact when not telling the truth. This is not the case with Asian people who avoid head touching for religious reasons but increase foot movements when lying.

The original Hand-to-Face Gestures

Covering the mouth when lying is commonly seen in children and can still be seen in adults as in Illustration 8. Lying increases nose sensitivity and may result in just a Nose Touch (Illustration 9). Covering the eyes with the hands stops us from looking at what we don't like seeing or don't believe and is the origin of the Eye Rub Gesture (Illustration 10). Tugging or Rubbing the Ear (Illustration 11) or Scratching the side of the Neck (Illustration 12) are also indicators that the person is uncertain or disbelieving about what is being said.

8.   **9.**   **10.**

85

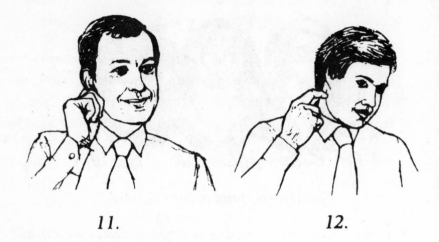

11.   *12.*

Some useful strategies

1. Always read hand-to-face signals in clusters and in context. Don't confuse an itchy nose with deceit.
2. Avoid Hand-to-Face gestures at all times during your presentation, as your audience will be less trusting. Practice in front of a video camera or a mirror to help you eliminate face touching.
3. If someone is using Hand-to-Face gestures during your presentation, try this -

"I can see you have a question - would you mind if I ask what it is?"
A stronger version is -
"Your Body Language tells me you have a question - would you mind if I ask what it is?"

Be cautious how you use this last question as it can sometimes seem affronting - it's used by professional interrogators!

POSITIVE BODY SIGNALS

1. The Head-Tilt:
We tilt our head when we are interested in what we see or hear. If your prospect is tilting, keep presenting. If his head straightens, wobbles or is dropped onto his chest, get involvement or change direction.

2. Hand-to-Cheek:
This shows a positive evaluation of your presentation. The hand rests on the cheek but does not support the head. The finger usually touches the temple. If the head begins to be supported by the hand, interest is waning.

3. Sucking Glasses:
A person may also suck a pen, pencil or even their own lips. This is a form of evaluation and can be seen when the person is trying to reach a decision. It can also be used to stall making a decision because the person feels justified in not answering while their mouth is otherwise occupied.

4. Leaning In:

We move closer to people and things we find interesting or attractive. This is not to be confused with the Starter's Position which looks similar but both hands are on the knees and the person looks like they are about to start a race, probably towards the door.

5. The Steeple:

This gesture can be read as a solitary gesture and it displays a cool, confident attitude. The question is, however, confident about what? Confident about going along with you? Confident about their own knowledge of the subject? Have they heard it all before? The context under which it is used will give you the correct answer.

6. Protruding Thumbs:

Thumbs can protrude from coat pockets, trouser pockets or on lapels and braces. Protruding Thumbs signal a superior attitude – confident and cool, similar to that of the Steeple gesture. It is unwise to use this gesture in front of your audience as it can also be read as a smug or arrogant attitude.

7. Both-Hands-Behind-Head:

Used almost exclusively by men it communicates an attitude of, "I know all about this – I've got all the answers." Try asking this man a question such as, "I can see you know something about this – would you care to give us your experience?" This can result in either cooperation or a debate, depending on the context in which the gesture is being used.

NEGATIVE BODY SIGNALS

1. Critical Evaluation:

This gesture is widely used and reveals critical thoughts by the listener. The index finger points directly up the cheek, the thumb supports the chin and the middle finger is beside or over the mouth. A question like, "What's your opinion?" can draw out the person's concerns.

2. Picking-Imaginary-Lint:

Imaginary-lint-picking reveals disapproval about what is being said. The person looks away while picking the imaginary lint or fluff. An approach such as "I can see you have a question" could work well with this person.

3. The Collar Pull:

When someone is silently angry, upset or being deceitful it causes a tingling sensation in the neck which gives the person the urge to pull the collar away from the neck. A question like "How do you feel about this?" could be appropriate.

4. Pain-In-The-Neck:

This expression perfectly describes what is happening here. Mounting tension or frustration causes the person to rub or slap the back of the neck to satisfy the tingling sensation that occurs when someone or something gives you a literal 'pain in the neck'. This is caused by the movement of the tiny erecta pillae muscles in the neck.

5. Slow Blinking:

This annoying gesture is used by a person who feels he is better, wiser, richer or smarter than you are and it is often accompanied with the raising up on the soles of the feet to gain height. The brain shuts out what it doesn't want to see by closing the eyes. This person may look upon you with contempt.

6. Leg-Over-Chair:

This has a combination of meanings – first, that the person feels relaxed and self-confident, particularly if it's not his chair; second, it's a form of territoriality because he stakes his claim with the leg over the chair. The overall attitude is that of relaxed indifference.

7. Straddling-A-Chair:

This is mainly a male gesture which sends a message of dominance or superiority. The back of the chair gives protection against a possible 'attack' and the Legs Spread is a classic male domination ploy. Never argue with the person who takes this position. Instead, get involvement or ask them to turn the chair around the right way.

8. Slow-Hand-Rubbing:

The speed of the handrub shows the person's likely emotions. Fast hand rubbing is done by a person who is feeling excited about the outcome for everyone concerned. Slow hand rubbing is used when the person expects to personally receive benefits or make money from the discussion.

A Typical Cluster

In this scene, the woman on the right has assumed the classic Critical Evaluation Cluster and the man on the left is using Open-Palms and leaning forward to try to draw her out. The man in the centre is using the Steeple and an aggressive leg position which reflects his confident, self-assured attitude.

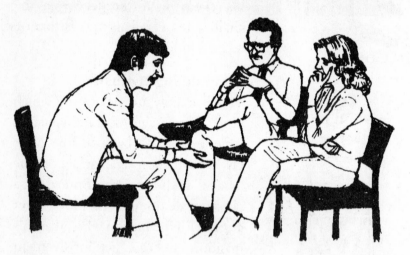

THE LAST WORD

Body language is like a jigsaw puzzle – most of us have many of the pieces but have never put them together to form a picture.

Always remember the Number One rule of Body Language – never interpret gestures in isolation, always look for clusters. Be sine to consider the context of all signals and acknowledge cultural differences.

Being able to read Body Language means being able to see the obvious in everyday situations.

Now look at the next illustration. What do you see?

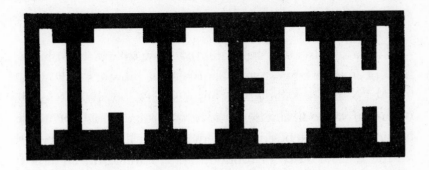

IN CONCLUSION

How many times have you heard someone say 'She's a natural' or 'He's a born salesman' when referring to a top-level networker?

You'll never hear a person described as 'a natural engineer' or 'a natural pharmacist' or 'a born doctor'. We know that these occupations are sciences.

A science is a skill or technique achieved by systematic study based on observation, experiment and measurement.

Top level networkers are not 'natural' or 'born'. Top level networking is a science – a learnable art – the same as any of the sciences. This book gives you some powerful techniques and shows you how to use them, how to measure and improve your progress and what to observe when dealing with people. The science of networking is a learnable skill that requires the same dedication, perseverance and practice as do all the sciences.

One of the greatest challenges networkers face on their journey to success is over-sensitivity to a negative response. When you use the techniques set out in this book, you will understand how every 'No' is, in fact, a positive step towards achieving your goals. Keeping your averages will prove this to you constantly.

This book discloses the secrets of 'how to' which for many, have been their biggest stumbling blocks. Now, it's up to you.

The Network Marketing business has evolved virtually overnight without fanfare or advertising and could eventually become the largest business system of them all. Its success relies on the referral-based distribution system and is driven almost entirely by the enthusiasm of its members. It is one of the most dynamic opportunities ever created by the mind of man.

This book has given you the keys to unlock the treasures in the system and propel you at great speed towards success. Everything in this book is proven and tested and gets immediate results. Everything will work, provided you do. There are no longer any excuses for not achieving the levels you want. So set your goals and go for it!

Allan Pease

Why not use Allan Pease as guest speaker for your next conference or seminar?

PEASE INTERNATIONAL PTY LTD

PO Box 1260, Buderim 4556, Queensland, AUSTRALIA
Tel: +61 7 5445 5600

Email: info@peaseinternational.com
Website: www.peaseinternational.com

Allan and Barbara Pease are the most successful relationship authors in the business. They have written a total of 15 bestsellers - Including 9 number ones- and give seminars in up to 30 countries each year. Their books are available in over 100 countries, are translated into 51 languages and have sold over 25 million copies. They appear regularly in the media worldwide and their work has been the subject of 9 television series, a stage play and a number one box office movie which attracted a combined audience of over 100 million.

Their company, Pease International Ltd, produces videos, training courses and seminars for business and governments worldwide. Their monthly relationship column was read by over 20 million people in 25 countries. They have 6 children and 5 grandkids and are based in Australia and the UK.

Also by Allan Pease:

DVD Programs
Body Language Series
Silent Signals Series
How To Be A People Magnet - It's Easy Peasey
The Best Of Body Language
How To Develop Powerful Communication Skills - Managing the Differences Between Men & Women

Audio Programs
The Definitive Book Of Body Language
Why Men Don't Listen & Women Can't Read Maps
Why Men Don't Have A Clue & Women Always Need More Shoes
How To Make Appointments By Telephone
Questions Are The Answers
It's Not What You Say

Books
The Answer
Body Language-How to Read others Thoughts by their Gestures
The Body Language of Love
Body Language in the Work Place
The Definitive Book Of Body Language
Why Men Don't Listen & Women Can't Read Maps
Why Men Lie & Women Cry
Why Men Want Sex & Women Need Love
You Can! People Skills For Life
Questions Are The Answers
Why He's So Last Minute & She's Got It All Wrapped Up
Why Men Can Only Do One Thing At A Time & Women Never Stop Talking
How Compatible Are You? Your Relationship Quiz Book
Talk Language
Get It Write

www.PeaseInternational.com